I0819267

ALSO BY JONAH MIXON-WEBSTER

Stereo(TYPE)

PROMISE / THREAT

PROMISE THREAT

POEMS

JONAH MIXON-WEBSTER

ALFRED A. KNOPF • NEW YORK • 2026

A BORZOI BOOK
FIRST HARDCOVER EDITION PUBLISHED BY ALFRED A. KNOPF 2026

Published by Alfred A. Knopf, a division of Penguin Random House LLC, 1745 Broadway, New York, NY 10019.

Library of Congress Cataloging-in-Publication Data
Names: Mixon-Webster, Jonah, 1988- author
Title: Promise/threat : poems / Jonah Mixon-Webster.
Other titles: Promise/threat (Compilation)
Description: First hardcover edition. | New York : Alfred A. Knopf, 2026.
Identifiers: LCCN 2025019836 (print) | LCCN 2025019837 (ebook) |
ISBN 9780593803066 hardcover | ISBN 9780593803073 ebook
Subjects: LCGFT: Poetry
Classification: LCC PS3613.I886 P76 2026 (print) | LCC PS3613.I886 (ebook) |
DDC 811/.6—dc23/eng/20250624
LC record available at https://lccn.loc.gov/2025019836
LC ebook record available at https://lccn.loc.gov/2025019837

penguinrandomhouse.com | aaknopf.com

Printed in Canada

1 3 5 7 9 10 8 6 4 2

For the dreamers, the believers, and the lovers

As one who dreams they are harmed,
and dreaming may wish that it were a dream,
therefore they long for the thing that is as if it were not.

—DANTE ALIGHIERI, *Inferno* (XXX; trans. Robert Pinsky)

I've done some dreaming in the nighttime, yes I have
Oh, but lately I've been dreaming in the daytime too

—THE MONTCLAIRS, "Dreaming's Out of Season"

CONTENTS

II

III

PROMISE / THREAT

Elsewhere

During those unconscious rituals,
I leave my body to become
a different person altogether.
I wear another face for the crowds
of butterfly people swarming past
and am now a stranger in my country—
in my head. What I bring with me
are memories of the unfamiliar
when some spirited malfunction knocks
me into the static between fantasies.

Almost always a new life of concrete
to explore until I find a cliff
or colosseum to fall from and the feeling
of falling, or the feeling of being shot, drives
me back into myself in this life. This *real* life
I share with you in this stolen earth
of stolen bodies. And the undertaking
pushes me back into the total dark of nowhere.

Into parallels of what I assume to be true.
Facts left over from muscle memory.
Lucidly, I pulled myself up the wall by my neck
with full intention. I crawled on the ceiling,
which I suppose was also my imagination
telling me something about control.
How we must all resist it at some point,
again and again and again
in our sleep.

Are you always yourself
in your dreams? I ask myself,
thinking I know the answer.
In reality, the only thing I believe
is that I am exactly where I think I am.
Here, _________ , hanging off the steep sloping steps
of a giant amphitheater, the quadrangle
of a half-lit schoolyard, a water coffin.

Elsewhere,
I swam in the dark.
I drank liquor to steady myself against the sun.
I sought after a breakfast of dead meat.
I swallowed sand and was set free.
I cried into everyone's hands.
I need to stand with you in this chaos
of make-believe, looking
for what's not already ruined.
I desire what I fear we will find.

I

Promise/Threat

I woke burying the memory of myself and myself chewing glass to a silent end unswallowing and I stood straight up pushing a finger behind the snag that caught my tongue on the sticking edge hung down from a corner slant atop the wisdom tooth now dead and my soft plunging breaks it into a scythe and what I recall from my sleep another mouth maybe turning and I bite my own hand thinking *pain is only perceived in the mind* says the mind of the dreamer who for once now woke feels nothing *perhaps* I say *then either all of it hurts or none of it does* which is how I come to find the blood and new tooth in my hand apart from the projection of my body I wrap the half molar in silk placing it under the slunk head of a man and make a selfish wish I blink and am somewhere else when what comes next is myself with some other figure committing an act in a parked Impala bound by the shadow a market throws in some buzzing daylamp I won't confess another thing yet somehow the screen on my device shatters making a shallow web my finger hits a sharp button burying a slice into the point I press my thumb into to squeeze from underneath the glass needle slowly pops from my flesh peeking out with its smile a beam of rose and silver garland hooking a peel of skin I nestle in my bite to pluck the thorn out becomes a bone plate I snap meat off of the chewing cracks a crown on the palatal wall filling my cheeks with eggshell scraping gum and sand against the animal in my mouth spreading over it now there is something I am trying to communicate here but I am muted by thirst the mind returns to the image in the dream and it is as if my eyes appear from the swinging doors of my throat and I look upon the double gate of stone yapping on the severed glass out of sleep I survey what remains of the tooth catching more blood in the organ my first warning of the coming rot warning of an intruder warning of the body itself—its own pillage

Reporting Live from the Ghetto of My Mind

Now that I lack the good   God given faith
to sleep at all   I refuse the slab bed
to haunt   the shadow limbs of streetlamps
with my singsong   happy laugh
lying inside another man's mouth
mudding crowds of lily spring through
a gap   in my gold teeth while a stream
of stop signs ricochet   slow bullets
toward the onerous mercy of the pollute
maddening silence   bisecting horn screech
young bulls rage in gutters pissy-drunk
from dissonance their Lincoln coin faces facing
doubled-up   styrofoam cups and pockets   shaken
empty for parking meters   and other drugs
and on this block   even the fiends got fiends
and I just stumped my toe   on a blunted stone
so now the branches of my body dangle off
the corners of a high soapbox   while I shout softly
I'm praying for a prayer   I'm coming to you live
from the corner of Shit Blvd. and Out o' Luck St.
with my monkey paws   clapping like sea leaves
to my drum-feet slushing slashing past the pigs
hiding beneath   dumpster bodies
and on the mirrored walls   the reviled image
of me and my sick slick silk self   like clockwork
the wounded moon in my mind reopens   like dead
skin on ripe fruit   like a hungry orifice   a hole
bricked up like a well of light   reflecting
every bloody corner   in the shape of shadows
in the shape of a galleria door   with arced pillars

and frames and stages holding the glass veil thinly
there are minds   within minds   within minds   here
at the bazaar   I bought and sold my favorite T-shirt
I bought and sold my brain   for pennies
to feed the stick-figure people of myself
screaming *give me*   myself   a tiny little beggar
begging for it all   begging for everything
anything for anything   *do you have anything?*
Anything?   *Anything?*
                                        Nothing?!

Transfigurations

To feed whatever hunger, I open my mouth not for food but for spirits with gentleman names: Jim Beam when I feel southern, Johnnie Walker when the music hits, Don Julio when feeling cross-cultural, Jose Cuervo when I'm feeling brave, Paul Masson when I feel dark as dark, Rémy Martin when feeling French and fancy, Uncle Nearest when feeling nostalgic, Augustus Bulleit when I'm nearing the end, Jack Daniel's when there's nothing and no one else. It is too obvious to say that I am meditating deeply on voids and consumption. So, I will only mention the birds from here on out. While drinking Crown I spot a cardinal and the coincidence is lost upon me. The red animal appears to be hungry as well darting from branch to pole to branch, its neck breaking to satisfy its beak. It catches a live object in its bird mouth and flies south I presume. Birds always seem to fly south as we're told. But I imagine the cardinal could have gone to the only home it knows and never leave again. It could have gone to look for its mother or father to open its bird mouth to say *look what I've found out in the world.* It could not be what I call it and be itself all the same. It could have gone to flock with other birds of the same feather to fly higher than ever before. It could have gone somewhere and started a new life. It could have died and been reborn as a rock. It could have died and been reborn as my brother squawking away at the morning business. It could have died and been reborn as a man asking me for my last cigarette in which I would give it knowing the bird is an animal like any other animal. Thirsty. Seeking. Starved.

The Negro Dreams of Fried Chicken

I am frying chicken at this very moment, two hundred and twenty feet in the air. In the back of my negro mind I think this is a kind of heaven or reparations for a violence I haven't accounted for yet. Though, what I mean to show you is that I am waiting for the chicken blood to turn black in the grease before I flip the whole wing on its side to brown a little more on the bottom. In some moment during my sleep, I'm sure I dreamt the negro dream of chicken in my negro hands a whole fantasy not entirely savage and consumed with picking bones between my teeth but in the way I imagine the whole nation running its fingers through my negro scalp to see if it's what everyone expects. Maybe you are simply picturing a false negro voice coming from a false negro body in your head and hopefully this causes us all to question what's really *real* now while I attempt to finish this perlocutionary act by telling you to smell the golden crispy fried chicken and the seasoned sea salt pepper onion flour and the fresh hot grease burning the black off the backs of my negro hands—it's real. You can eat it up too.

Dollar Straight / Dollar Box

The draw, an easy money pickup we all knew came
true as God by how we prayed on it. Monday through
every day, the same morning-midday-evening ritual.
Four-way for sure luck. A certainty, three digit of softer odds.

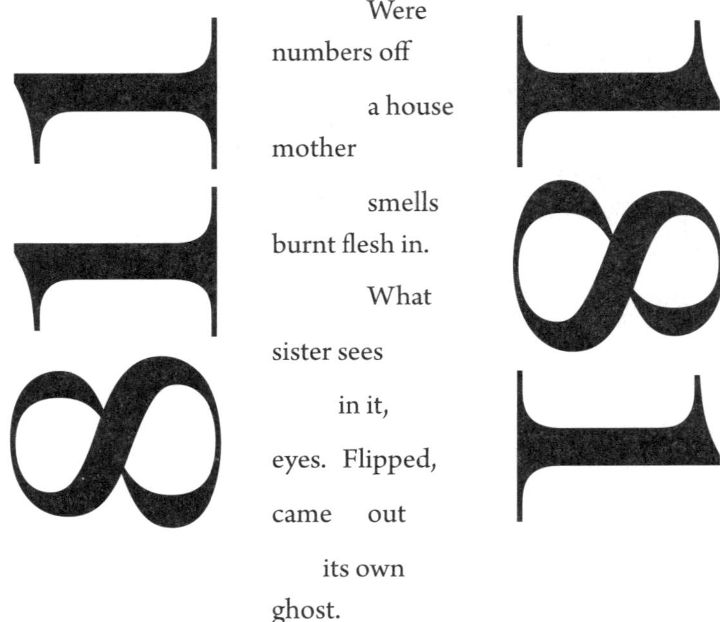

Were
numbers off
a house
mother
smells
burnt flesh in.
What
sister sees
in it,
eyes. Flipped,
came out
its own
ghost.

My first hit after choosing the pets.
Make the wager in Michigan,
maybe drop in Illinois.
Mama says, *Play what you need.*
Dreambook says the number "father"
appears as on the slip. Neither comes.

There is a neighborhood legend of my young
toddler-fevered mouth shouting the winning number. They say,
Man, we all hit four days in a row until you got better.
I haven't been right since.

Remember that number.

In third grade, light-skin Brittney
asks, *What happened? Yo' mama hit
the lottery or somethin'? Because you ain't
never had Nautica before.*
She did.

Then the same number, even, paid my court fees—kept me out of jail!

1918

*Never say your numbers
out loud though—everybody'll be rich!*

I recall past plate numbers, overdo the math again
in my head, add the forms to feel the weight of it.
Prime sums stuff gullets with guessing, composites
allude to a relation of parts, other phantasms.
Coincidence means "pay attention." Meaning, *Scared*
money don't make money—

DNM273 6
HEM782 35YR1DR
0
BOS206 6
BZJ1249
WYT7805
4 FLT6901
2343VR MXV913
7
KFR702 G1V UP
3

If you spend with the numbers man, one spot let you put down
for a nickel on the wheel. Then you can win enough to buy yourself a new
ticket. Birthday comes out straight in the midday, not a dollar on it.
They watching you! a man at the machine says before feeding his pockets.
They know when you play, what you play, when you don't play.

A mirror gives you the obvious of what will drop next—
Time, place, a date, the nearest name, the absence of expectation
notwithstanding. *You can't win, if you don't play.* The man says while feeding his pockets,
And well hell, if I was in your shoes, I'd bet my last dollar too.

Reinvention

Under the summer bucket hat of my past life I was a bulldog walking in slow heat Sweat beating up my face reminded me of rain dancing on the blurred edge of my periphery My jaw strung out with my bottom lip hung in dry heave panting hard to catch the wind And I had no other way to protect myself from myself In the sun's cruel nature I walked toward an oasis of blackness which was a dim mirage I saw in the penumbra of my brims' shade And there was no other method to hide from the heat and the heat of white weather gazed strangers and the confusion I feel when they all look at me that way So I became afraid of both the sun and the eyes staring at me through the daylight looking glass But in all actuality I have nothing to hide or nothing to hide from truly Not even this knighthead of nappy brush Sloping like dark cotton stalks blooming like a mouth giving you its black tongue to pluck I must have done something worth forgetting I must have made something up to reveal my shame

Snitch

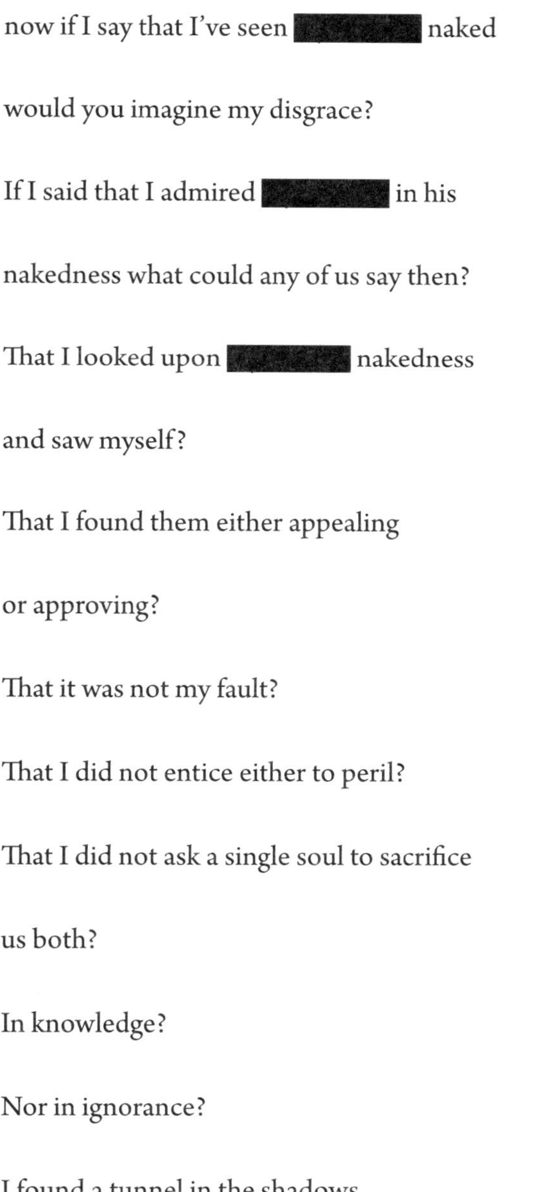

now if I say that I've seen ████ naked

would you imagine my disgrace?

If I said that I admired ████ in his

nakedness what could any of us say then?

That I looked upon ████ nakedness

and saw myself?

That I found them either appealing

or approving?

That it was not my fault?

That I did not entice either to peril?

That I did not ask a single soul to sacrifice

us both?

In knowledge?

Nor in ignorance?

I found a tunnel in the shadows.

They found their own in the deep

light that begins in the hole of death

and all the birds agree.

I know your secrets

but will not use them against you.

You know my secrets but hold them

as a weapon you could strike me with

at any time.

But I am unafraid.

I am not scared of my own life

nor am I searching for it.

I hold light in my own grave

and rise again to see and say nothing at all.

Inchoate Chatter

T. S. Eliot House
Gloucester, MA

The veil is thin here as the total dark
and stone ramble against the rush
of tree whisper and the trees
draw me to their memory. A sign informs
that I am in "America's Oldest Seaport."
I'm sure there is something to be said
about that but for now I deny
the invitation. I also deny the *beauty*
of this place made a place only
by the history it must conceal.
Hidden absence, moreover presence
undone. Someone must always leave,
so someone must always remain.
Derrida, ventriloquizing Marx, reminds me
that due to great violence, our sense
of time is disjointed. And I assume
that our sense of place is disjointed along
with it. The sea ferries' buoyant light
shreds the clouded drapery to reveal a message
to be read with a cold open map of night,
"America's Oldest Seaport."
I'm sure there is something to be said
about that. There is also something
to say about the brown waves of fog
Eliot once mused over and the lyrical
pareidolia to follow. Surely, he imagined it
as clear as I am imagining myself
in his home. Rattling the shades,
rifling through his cupboards, helping

myself to his drink, relieving myself
on his curtains, tiptoeing loudly over
the eerie plywood of would-be servants.
I wonder if Eliot would still turn his ear
to the basements of others, his eyes
to the trampled road. When all he would
need to know is here—in the right hand
of his youth. I imagine what he calls
the *nigger drawl* of his voice mixed
with echoes of luxury plastered across
this attic with his poor, forlorn face peeking
through a mask worn with his mouth alone.

We Might Crash Out in This Poem

I see our face, a seed pressed against the glass against
the concrete. The water or gas spilling toward us
as we lie there as it is much easier for us to wait
for our heads to catch fire or to scrape against the ass
of a man laid atop our ear than it is to begin crying
at the wreckage. His sit bones lift through the window
of our passenger's new moonroof. We eat the pavement
and I hold his holy body toward salvation. Imagine,
three black men born to die dying, slowly.
Who knows what we had to drink or had to think
to get to this point of wanting suicide like Englishmen?
The French call it *L'appel du vide* or "the call of emptiness."
The Germans call it *Selbstmord* or "self-murder." The Arabians say,
اسْتِشْهاديّ or "watch me take myself out." The Wolof whisper,
Xaru or "no more suffering." The Japanese, again, say, 腹切り
or "we deserved it." To the older man in the other car,
I apologize. I did not mean it. I did not intend to get you caught
in the wreck of my reckless self and the other one wishing to live also.
The way I wish I saw it was us all making it to our destination.
Something that *would* make the news—"Three black men lived today
despite an accident, one was deathless, the other one spoke but couldn't
breathe much but he's conscious now, also. They are still products
of their environment of this moment." Maybe you too wagered your death
against another life. Or wanted a way or a reason out of your troubles. But here
we are, talking loud and long through the streetlights about who is more ready
to live. Yes, there is another plan we must fulfill. I dreamt of bigger fish
last night and blocks stuffed with numbers on its side. I remember
your face. You, looking at me wishing us life. The both of us
wishing us more healing. Well, my brother, we already have it.

I May Leave a Piece of Myself Here Just to Haunt You

And if when I'm gone
        I don't fly but sink
to find root mud to find
        you in seagrass in my new
navel sunflower legs
        opening again and again
to find the light of myself
        stuck to you in eyeglow
ghost circus sideshow
        maybe when we leave
we finally know we can't
        for now I'm tired of my body
full of bloodriddles my face
        another puzzle to solve
after everything else falls flat
        in place where it fits
to a sky where it doesn't belong

From One Nightmare to Another

Where are you tonight nightstalker? Are you warm in your space of loneliness where you keep company with ghosts in the mouth of frost teasing me to be a victim? I hope you hear my voice through the terror, that you see my faces in your dreams. When I said I wasn't always The Boogeyman, you said you weren't always Jeepers Creepers, I thought we understood each other then. What's an urban legend to an urban legend? I understood you when you were in my closet car faking sleep with my snake hand on your chest of feathers. Maybe that was the only way I thought we could be close enough. Through horrific traps set for us and a mask of dust. I paid the sandman a visit today. Spoke of you. Asked for the future through a mirror of smoke and for a pipe to feed us twilight. I love being mad with you. Scraping strange money together to make the world pay for its crimes. Showing our naked bodies in the daylight as a sign of things to come. Someone in my head says that *hell* is short for *help*. That *sell* is short for *self*. Now I'm beginning to think we bought off the real devils through red bedsheets and white crumbs stuffed into canine snouts snuffed snapping foam from their thirst and fiendish jaws with dark rings that Virgil guides us. When you turn your back I see blood through your jacket and you walk through the minds of city folk with only socks on to make me fall back in love. I see the dirt on your collar the same color as my skin. What sticks to us, sticks to us. What names we give our darkness live on in the light and make the people whisper. When they see us together next time, let them watch.

I Seek Out an Expert Opinion on the Nature of Dreams

And you know what? They know just as much as we all do.
    That they appear
    from the most sensitive parts of our brain.
Tiny impressions reproduced. New information
synthesized into old systems. Exits. Entrances. Reconciliation.
    Of the two. Keys unlocking what manifests automatically.
    Everything all at once
    and nothing at all.

    Eva tells me she dreamt of the south vanishing.
The whole thing. No more and nothing. The Floridian Palms, the Georgia Pine,
Mississippi Oaks, Weeping Widows in the Carolinas, the Delta itself.
    Gone. I see what she says as she says she woke up screaming.
    If you scream out of your sleep, it means something.
    If you talk in your sleep, it means something.
    If you choke in your sleep, it means something.

    The patient's eyes have fallen.
    Let's watch the heartbeat wired for sound.
    Sensors check for rhythm in time
    with the patient's body indicating a phantom through the epoch
of a dream. Already before the experiment the hypothesis
is pronounced. I'm sick and sugar-free in the daytime, sugar-free
    in the night. I love the look on a man's face in the ethers
    while the black lens of my eye registers ecstatic colors.

    El tells me I was sleepwalking through his home in Houston.
    That I started doing laundry. I filled the basket
    with water and soap but not with clothes. I filed

  into a space I don't remember. Maybe I'm playing
  with fire. Performing half chores to go back to my couch
of sand where I find a different labor. Listening to people telling me
I did something I don't remember doing which is a kind of dream also.
  My mother tells me I brought the vacuum
  in the house and attributes it to water and I feel blamed for forgetting.
I shoot rockets from my mouth. A dream of a new song to drown out her voice.
I feel a spirit and feed it gunpowder. Now we're both choking
  on the same thing I saw in my blood.

You Got Spirits in You

The spirit of anger the spirit of fear the spirit of loneliness the spirit of guilt the spirit of love the spirit of night the spirit of day the spirit of shame the spirit of today the spirit of the past the spirit of the future of the Spirit the spirit the Spirit the spirit of ain't this about a bitch the spirit of my dead dead people the spirit of where did we go wrong? The Spirit of I tried! The spirit of alcohol the spirit of cigarettes the spirit of a saving grace the spirit of oh hell naw not today the spirit of I see you family the spirit of where all this crack come from? The spirit of love the spirit of sex The spirit of where the food at?! The spirit of a fool The spirit of a scholar The Spirit of a woman the spirit of mistrust the spirit of not today how bout tomorrow? The Spirit of ain't that about enough? The spirit of a gladiator the spirit of a Spirit the spirit of you and the spirit of me the spirit of don't you know better? The Spirit of I know that spirit the spirit of c'mon man tell me something! The Spirit of sleep the spirit of hunger the spirit of rage the spirit of being left out the spirit of yeah now that's the spirit! The spirit of hands the spirit of fire the spirit of shit the spirit of quiet or the spirit of quit the spirit of die today and again tomorrow the spirit of smoke of drink or breath the spirit of being in the dark the spirit of a man the spirit of a coke and a smile the spirit of shut up and shut up and up and up and up

Lost and Found

Where's the office? Who's in charge? Who do I need to speak to? Where's the bucket? Where's the bin? Where's the tote? Where's the box? Where's the shelf? Where's the bill? Where are my pants? Where's my draws? Where is my picture-day picture with me before a blue backdrop in a blue polo shirt though I never knew how to play polo? Where's Marco? Where's Polo? Where's my heart? Where's the feeling I'm looking for? Where's the place where I left my shoes? My socks? My mouth? My body? Where is it? Did I leave it behind to go to the far off? Where's my mother tongue? Man, now where's my history? Where's the books that hold my history? The books that tell me where I am and that tell me where I'm going next? Where are my ears? Where's the ashes I left and the Bible I left and the words that flew out of my mouth with somewhere to go? Where's my damn keys? Where did I leave my phone? Or where did my phone leave me? Where did I put my soul? What body did I leave it hanging out with? Where did I last see it? What were my last steps? Where did I put it? Now where's the bottle? I thought I put it under the seat. I thought I put it in a place to come back to. Where did I put my rifle? I had it right here between my teeth and promised to return. Where did I put my love? Where did I last see it? Where do I remember seeing it last? What did I do with it? Where did I put that last slice of bread? I remember hiding it from myself. I remember hiding it from the rats. I thought I hid it from the rats. Did they find it? Did I find it? Did they ask me for it and did I give it to them? Did I say something I didn't mean? Did I mean it? I probably meant it at the time but now I want to take it back. Am I an Indian giver? Do I give things then take them back? Am I American? Am I America? Where's my damn apples? Where's that one apple I wanted to eat? Where's the sweetest thing I ever known? Where's my mama? Where's my daddy? Where did them little kids' babysitter go as I made them a sandwich in that strange apartment that I had a drink and a smoke inside of and thought about how I would never leave three babies alone to fend for themselves but somebody did? Did they know what they did? Where did my life go? I won't beg for it to come back, but I wonder. Man these are real questions. Where my mind go? Did I lose it somewhere on the path God laid out for me? Did I even know God during this time? Did I feel like there was no God and I went traveling along anyway? Did I think I would figure it all out? Where is my damn keys? Aw shit, now where's my wallet? Where's my phone? Where's that one video I don't want nobody else to see but me and God? Where's God? Where did

I leave it? I had God right here in my back pocket. I could pull it out at any time. I could say what I wanted and would find an ear to listen, long as I had God in my back pocket. Now it's gone somewhere. I don't even remember where I left it. Where is the bottle? I thought I put it under the seat. I thought I put it on the side of the house we were sharing. I thought I grabbed it, put it to my lips, and put it back again. I thought it was right here. I thought I hid it in this sentence. Oh wait, here it is. Okay, I feel better now. But where is the line I drew in the sand? The line I drew and told everyone not to cross. I guess I crossed it myself so now it's not there anymore. Where's my phone? Where's the person that took my phone? I don't want to hate that person just to get my phone back. It's okay. They already know what's in it. Where is my ██████ phone? Did everybody see it already? Did I get found out with my one and only secret? And where are my secrets? Are they in the streets? Are they in somebody's mouth? In somebody's ears? In somebody's heart? In a soul that don't know that my secrets are a curse? I hope everybody's okay with my secrets because I'm not. Where are my damn secrets? Those are mine and I want them back. Never mind. Keep them.

Weapons a Thought Could Wield

In the word of the mind, the mind of the word—murder, a simple premise, quick utility, pistol or cane, a wood or any metal, new money for old rope, a nail for the body, field for the coffin, a simple premise—inevitability, a shout and a gather, a rubbernecking, a knowing, slew occupations, knife in a bread box, missiles in the hamper, bombs in the basement, a trap, the catch, a rumorer, inevitability, a simple premise—what becomes of a mind becomes of a body, zero thought, something hard, something harder, a knowing, time and place, depth and proximity, a piece of piss, the portent, a simple premise—murder, a look at the waste, a thing to hold and a thing to be held on to, a mother's purse, your father's pockets, armories of the state, mundane ornaments, a cross for your hands, a cross for your back, the forgetting, inevitability, black sheet for burial, daylight for discovery, tokens of vengeance, a war for meaning, a war for peace, the simple premise—want. For whom? For what? What purpose? What reason? None.

II

Territory

Sometimes I sit just like this. Alone. Dusting off the smoke of my sleep. Wondering where I had gone only to find myself back here. I remember there was a field where I went. A home to explore the memories of. I laid in the Woodlawn of my other life and now wish to return. Other nights I sleep with my head standing like a puddle of rain. Take a gargled breath and wake up choking on my spit. Sometimes I sleep on my back waiting for someone to come find me and hide the evidence. Tell everyone I died naturally and with respect. And not with my hand on my crotch. No magazine nor film to document my pleasure unlasting. That I didn't soil myself in the process. No, not a stain in sight.

this new world turns like a water mill
on a red-clay river where I find myself
spitting dirt rocks through tall-bladed cattails
cutting the heat of tractor engines lighting up
honkytonks with a mob full of ghost faces
white as dove feathers   yet again I am unafraid
as the shrieks scurry into backfields leading
to a somewhere and the carrying on of a slung
tire swinging over a burning bridge   wait
on someone's front yard dandelions lie
with their fluff half-blown   flat breath
over glass jaws   strumming straw   wind chime
whistles between teeth   tuning forks kicking up
dust in the world's melody a sudden creek
rolling me through the rushes the penny-flame
sun falling all at once like a cliché like autumn
leaves slow   dancing to the ground or horses
running from water midstream running
running into the scene I follow toward the hills
stacked like cannons without ammunition
without a soul to steal   or save

In this horror   I am reincarnated
into the bullet which marks my passing   and this is what I know it means
        first: language is the original trigger,
                                  focus, scope, and a target for every weapon
                                        which is to say:
                                  I found myself, again, in an unfamiliar place
                        running   from shibboleths when
someone said *Get that nigger!*   so I shot
                                                                    the first one I saw
in the mirror
with an immanent slug   which means:
recursively,   someone is already in the image of dying or
dead
which is also to say: there must be a certain survival mechanism
playing out   meaning:
                                  another sad thing already   meaning:
alright, here it is—   the bullet   my mouth   the simple machine
                                  pointed at itself
meaning: saying the wrong thing here will get you killed
                                  now, I hope to never speak again.

I subsist in a dead land
where shrunken heads sit
in glass jars dingy
on roundabout hills
to bleed in split tongues
the language of a borrowed ear.
Be sure to say nothing,
they slaughter the unintelligible.
But lie around the beating drum
and we'll give you summer.
Flagrant foreign thoughts
are held by a false nothing.
Us natives are too contemporary
for your modern song.
The sounds are tenuous
compared to your breath
of broad strokes.
Do you hear the cymbals?

Where it was is when / There are wood panels all over / and I am a collective member of a white simulation in blackface / There is a man with a low fade who is my friend without his locs / Never a mirage / Never my eye casting out to itself in memory / There is a fight between the races / Water in the tiger's mouth / A window / Twin slate moons huddle on the horizon / an oceanic circus of gray-light / A lion in a bubble / Now, all is on the surface / In the back, two blond women sit on the floor while praying to the dead / We think this is the reason why we're all here / Him, the white man sitting next to the one without locs / Unleashes his mouth / A backwards tongue gaped in riddle / In a kind of future-speak / Saying what sounds like: *Is us behind us is each is a door, is each a phantom, is each a pool, is each is a broken river looking back* / Everyone is a frozen statue and won't say anything when I shake them / I lift the shade behind the lids of all eyes / and every time / in each, I see the same child.

I finally find a ride out of the made-up made-up city. I bend every corner to find the way out, an exit ramp or entrance to an overpass to take me out of anywhere I remember. On the east wing of the city a twenty-foot fence causes me to rebound against another corner. On another path toward the west, the same fence. Apparently, I am trapped in two places at once. The car banks on a hill and stalls out. I don't remember anything else worth retelling.

I wait for light to wake me but find myself slumbering past my appointment. I am late this morning, which might as well be dusk. I have missed fulfilling my responsibility. I was supposed to be in a classroom. Teaching a young world about the old, about the new that's coming. How we must end the prophecy before it is settled. But I rise from the longest night of my life. Now I wish to either sleep forever or never again.

I don't know where I am this time. I don't want to be my own pallbearer. Helping to lower my body to its grave. I've seen what happens between infernos and paradises. Purgatory is not colorless. I beg the face of my mother to listen and her face stretches into a cry.

I pay a psychic to tell me what these recurring dreams mean for my daily life of consciousness. I mention the PTSD in real life. She says, *You have to let them shoot you in the dream so you can truly live when you wake.*

III

Back to Life / Back to Reality

After Soul II Soul

The real poem is the life I'm writing.
I don't want to hear any more blues today.
I am trying to remember my reason for living.
And what I mean to announce to the world,
in a sense, that it's something about being
in the world. Every speck of dirt,
the feeling of thirst
that makes you think, naturally.

Moreover, Does the Truth Still Speak

I have some knowledge of wicked things
but I do not wish to bear the whole fruit thereof.
As a tree of gold do I see myself grow.
A harvesting of olives and no parables
to confuse you with.
Now do I think of the worm that becomes
the snake that becomes a dragon that becomes
a snare that feasts
on the flesh of nature?
The fowl caught in the teeth
of the crocodile?
Yet escape is what I know.
That a revelation is only a revelation
to the revolutionary. But are we all doomed
to the simple act of fear? Fleeing. Fighting.
Shut-up whispers in our bones?
Heralds of no cheer bristling through the branch
where the leaves have not grown?
Are we lost in the making of ourselves?
Hearing not the voice of wise winds fluting
the truth? There must be more to learn for us all.
More to battle for and be buried with.

A Regret of Newness

For Tyrone Williams

We've survived the prophecy of our demise.
Our heart still beats, we're still here dreaming,
thinking of our good friend who has passed
without a word from us though we felt the need
to say something and mean it. I mean really
mean it. Nothing is simple these days. The day
turned its ruins to night. The night turned
its treasure into the day. While we try to reconcile
our death wishes with the fact we are still above ground.
Dead people talk to us in our sleep. We talk to them
in our dreams. Nothing is ever the same again.
There is nothing else to say. Our last memory
is already written. Our mouths are closed forever.

This is not a poem about death. I am writing
about how to live. How we are alive but feel
as if we're dead already. The dead remind us of that.
The living remind us of how we're dying slow deaths.
Someone whispers in our ears at the threshold, spoiling
our prayers. Last rites should come from a single soul. Unfettered.
A wish that blows the candle out. A flame that guides
us through the door to another life. A breath in the deep
that falls for the finale. Our friend taught us how to do it.

To cross the mind and figure everything else out.
To be alive, though dead. To be. To know
that something is not complete until it is complete.

To find more language in the gap between worlds. In between
what was said and what wasn't. To want to quit but stay
lively in the quiet hours of morning. To see a bird and know
what the bird says and what the bird means.
We got a new angel today. We got something
to look forward to. We get a new life.

Daydream for My Other Selves

I listened and had no silence in me
I welcomed what I had heard
with emptied-out skulls
in the spiritual pocket
in the not that sky is
I had the bright moons
of my fingernails
in the night
I had the blues—
the body of cut-up
made the mouth

made a sea of domes:
one planet for thunder
two planets for rain
I heard the dead speak
a cry aping crosses
the outer edge of my lip
caught in sand—
cathedral tower
—throats of heat

My Child, My Child

I do not know how to protect you
now that you are gone Somewhere
inside of me The people say do not
linger on your sight for too long
or I may lose myself also
But I'm waiting for you to teach me
a new lesson about joy and fearlessness
I'm learning how to be your parent
now that I have only your memory to correct
I trace the scar on our knee and call you brave
I see the scar on our forehead and think
of how you removed those stitches yourself
You are my favorite boy a son my father wishes
he could have loved as I love you without separation
or a mirror to divide us I love you
how I think a child needs to be loved With a smile
and cinnamon rolls and strawberry yogurt
I sneak into the bathroom for you to eat
while you are bathing in the water
watching *Good Times* I wish
I could have given birth to you alone
Immaculate and gleaming through the gap
of your baby teeth Then maybe the world
would know a miracle when they see one
When they see you and ask where did you come from
Who is your father Who is your mother
And you would point to me as one and the same
and I can be overjoyed with you
and pleased with myself as well alone

A Cruelty of Longing

With John Farmer

I

I was trying hard to cling to
some other thought: I want
to write myself
away and back to you

in the present
—all the words
come out wrong
when I'm trying not to shatter.

II

Come smoke me
with your body
in the cool mist
and bind our little parts

of speech with something lovely.
Whatever it's going to be
is what I need to know.

Please, under no circumstances,

speak of love.

III

Put something to my lips
numb it all—
a forsaking
I feel you
    taste as fancy does.

                                        Can I catch it? In a flower?

IV

Today,
there's nothing to write about.
This evening passed as usual
but still my body asks for it—

I've been trying to find
a new mouth
in the cruel night of clouds
dim from end to end

                                                            as the heart

          or a leaf.

V

O
                    how I want to eat up
                                                    all these acts
                              of gorgeousness—

truth is,
I am lonely
for a little light
to come down and touch me,
but I look up
and have no desire left for *this* world.

Please, under no circumstances,

speak of love

A Process of Wondering Which Begs Me to Question

how love makes us want
a thing we don't want
how it makes you want a shotgun
or a whistle to blow
to want love to bite, chew us up,
and spit us out into something
pretty and purposeful, maybe
love is a ghost we called a séance for
we sit around the table waiting for love
to answer to our magic
knock once for yes twice for no
and no knock comes
neither does a whisper
and now we are outside waiting for smoke
to fall from the clouds as a sign
that our voices were heard in the mirror
we chanted spells into for renewal
an awakening my heart is
a dog in a kennel barking for release
for a wind to blow the door off
the cage and run

Me and Those Dreamin' Eyes of Mine

After D'Angelo

If I had the chance, I'd cover them and hide
from your beauty lest it smite me on the brow
of my labor.

In the margins of sight you appear in shapely form
and looking as beautiful as ever in your worlds
of discovery and new questions.

Who are you today, my love? In what new country
do you feed your people? What are you made of,
honey? My love?

I am years late and millions short of feeling worthy.
You are the money in my eyes, true treasure
of spirit and endless.

Old-world traditions, seasonal winds calling me
out of my pit, a sunshine crescent moon smile
of beauty of pain of beauty.

How long should this last, my love? How many tears
do I turn to language in my chamber
of alchemy?

I can smell you also. Taste you, even, and I'm hooked.
I should remain silent but must tell the world
of how I imagine this going.

Find me at this address I made up in my head
with those eyes on the map. It's not home yet
of course.

But you can make it that when you get there.
Your eyes spell out fantastic news.
I could read them each day. Forever.

Bottomless Hearts Cry Out Our Names, O Love

In end, is giving
fit for the three shelter shapes
tricked to the roof of your mouth.

Hands are pallet and enough wind
in smolder jaw
to run the tongue in everything.

New spring shows love as a fifth season,
lifting out the roof of God's
                    godhead to heap up more than need:

The article of my own well for water
which I swallow and all becomes good and willing.

A gratitude of flood fingers, constantly holding on to warmth.
Withstanding heat and no torrential positions of mud-brain interactions.
                                        selfless chagrin, twinned
light ray just barely blinding my eyes but still dear nonetheless.
Take tips as love snatching off the frays of your pleasant ghost at the middle of it all.

On bring the heat, rainflower, and the never knowledge of death.
Unbled. Unsplit.

On the Sleeping Floor

I dream your mouth is a catacomb for rest
I dream your mouth is food for the hungry
I dream your mouth is a silver bullet
I dream your mouth is a firepit, is a lake
I dream your mouth is a Byzantium crystal and I am too poor to own it
I dream your mouth is a two-headed coin playing for keeps
I dream your mouth is a corridor with eight pathways, is a broken gate
I dream your mouth is a flytrap, but I am no moth
I dream your mouth is a starship / come take me up tonight / and don't be late
I dream your mouth is a lit candle
I dream your mouth is a citadel
I dream your mouth is a false mirror
I dream your mouth is a light tower of seven pillars
I dream your mouth is its own planet going through retrograde
I dream your mouth is glitter gorging on the dim night
I dream your mouth is a god and I pray to it when it is dark and I am lonely
I dream your mouth is a festival of grief and I am one of the dead
I dream your mouth is what keeps me from rising on the third day
I dream your mouth is a dram and I forget what it all means
I dream your mouth is my mouth
and they both lie here together, smiling—stuck

An Attenuated List of Things I Find in My Bed upon Waking

. half faces buried in cotton
. a foreign body
. remnants of many feasts
. a switchblade
. blood from the back of my head on the pillow
. blood from my sleep in the covers
. amorphous gunk
. tiny hairs of an insect
. an insect
. animal eyes atop my head
. string in my mouth
. a book with pissed-on pages
. snack wrappers that feel like a type of silk
. a pissed-on pissed-off lover
. a flattened cup of nothing
. two and a half uneaten cookies
. leftover cake
. animal bones
. a new nightscar
. Someone's father
. Someone's husband
. Someone

This Fantasy Has No End and Now I'm Stuck in It, Freakishly

My favorite part is when the screen goes blank
and there is only your whimpering voice on the record.
Where I can't remember what happens next.
I could imagine it to call to mind a kind of being one.
The rabbit in my ear telling me to jump in it.
The frog in my throat saying lick into the far winds.
The camel, the birds, the daylily, the rosemary,
the candlelight, its heat, the light, the endless
grass where I see us. Tell me nothing, my love.
The world has taught me enough. Told me who I am,
who you were, and who you are now. What I have not
spoken of is the screen like the glass of a crystal ball
I look through seeing us with my heart in your lap.
My favorite fragrance of déjà vu or jamais vu or déjà rêvé,
whatever name I could use to say you are the place
I can't get to. I can't help but return and beg.

Picking Fruit in One Dream and Eating It in the Next

i hold the strawberry
in one hand
shift it to the other
in this hand
the strawberry feels
pleasing i could eat
the strawberry or
i could leave it

for the sun
the strawberry plucks
itself from my mouth
invites me to wait
for the right time
now i want to share
the strawberry with you
so the taste finds us both

Twilight

I awoke in the new millennium
to find my honey already hooked
to it and cocked
quick in a black arm
wracked with mad faces
bleating out of each wound
a siren screaming as if each sore
were the speakerbox of mourning
        each sound its own trace
of an opalescent end.

Help Me Name It

My pretty love is a glutton
of and for punishment.
It begs me to crack the whip
and break its back.
To call it dirty names.
To abandon it and return
to hurt in equal measure.
What I hurt hurts me to the core.
What I leave leaves me as well.
Two backs to lie against the wall
of one another in one bed
so the rear bones rattle like vines
against the brick of winter.
My love wants the cold shoulder.
My love wants what it wants.
My love wants to not be wanted at all.
And I try my best to abuse it
as it needs a wound to make it,
make it make sense. My love,
what else must we gain in pain?
What bloody sacrifice must we offer
the fire to watch it work itself to dust?
From smoke must we forge
a home without wood or Sheetrock?
Nor the savior of the cherrybark
blossoming to make us a roof?
Help me make us a place my love
to call and call it
what we have yet imagined.

Mysterious Island

Meet me on mysterious island . . .
set your imagination free.
I will be there waiting for you
Received: May 18, 2022, 11:31 p.m.

I'm on my way, paddling wings
through an ocean-bucket of stars
to get to you. I keep my love fresh
in a basket of cherries I've picked
in your name. I lift the fog between us
with a mouth of fire. A genie lamp
for a head. A dance of dragonflies circling
the light. I'm bringing sand to the floating
beach, flowers to our secret garden,
waters to cleanse your feet.

Rising Moons in the Needles of Trees Bring Us Water

The light continues to wrestle the dark
in the squared circled hearts of haters
and lovers alike. There's a matter
in the sky that casts its lot of moonlight
where my eyes are kept. Every vision
is a fact yet I shouldn't speak too much
of the shadows following me down the hall
lest they hear my fear and keep track.
So where does joy go when we suffer?
Where does pain go when we are healed?
Must they exist together always in the void
of what goes unseen and untouched?
If you ruled the world what would you find first?
Endless space to conquer? Food for the hungry?
A light of your own to shine?

Let's hide in the mounds of dirt
waiting for light to find its promise.
In dirt there is no threat
besides getting dirty, besides
growing seeds from the mud
of the mind where you find
a flower to blow your breath
into sparking flames of desire
in your heart for softness and new
silk to make yourself a robe,
make yourself a rug, make yourself
anything you wish even a wish
you grant to yourself only.

If we find no more light in the world
then where have our eyes gone?
If it is all ruined and readied
to build up a new destruction,
then what does that say about our desire?
The trees work in the wind to create
nighttime melodies. The wind works
with water to urge the world
toward its destiny. The water works
with the rock to make new space
peaceful and steady. Nature makes
a wondrous team even in its terrifying force.
In the sky there is always light,
even in the dark, even in the day.

NOTES

"I Seek Out an Expert Opinion on the Nature of Dreams" uses lines inspired by Juicy's "Sugar Free."

"Territory" uses lines inspired by Chaka Khan's "Roll Me Through the Rushes" and Tower of Power's "Don't Change Horses (in the Middle of a Stream)."

"Daydream for My Other Selves" is a cento including lines from Jeff Clark, Peter Waterhouse, and Rigoberto González.

"A Cruelty of Longing" was written in collaboration with the poet John Farmer.

"On the Sleeping Floor" contains a line from "You Are My Starship" by Norman Connors (featuring Michael Henderson).

The title of "Picking Fruit in One Dream and Eating It in the Next" is inspired by Tom Raworth's poem "You've Ruined My Evening/You've Ruined My Life."

ACKNOWLEDGMENTS

"Promise/Threat" (originally published as "The Promise of Threat") and "Rising Moons in the Needles of Trees Bring Us Water" (originally published as "Rising Moons in the Needles of Trees Bring Me Water"), *The Yale Review*

"Transfigurations," *Zócalo Public Square*

"The Negro Dreams of Fried Chicken" and "Inchoate Chatter," *Indiana Review*, Afroforrealism Folio

"Dollar Straight / Dollar Box," "Snitch," "Moreover, Does the Truth Still Speak," "A Regret of Newness," and "My Child, My Child," *Obsidian: Literature & Arts in the African Diaspora*

"Weapons a Thought Could Wield," *Harper's Magazine*

"Territory" (various excerpts), *Southern Indiana Review*, Academy of American Poets *Poem-a-Day*, and *Shenandoah*

Thank God for the gift and responsibility of being a writer and for blessing me with the task of writing this collection.

Thank you to my mother, Carolyn J. Mixon, for dealing with the haze and giving feedback to these poems. To my father, Moses W. Webster, I hope you're resting in peace, and thank you for loving me, forgiving me, accepting my forgiveness. Thank you to all of my family and friends who have done their best to love me during some of the troubling processes of grappling with life and producing this work. Thank you to my compadres who have supported me with this project with your generous feedback: Nabila Lovelace, Airea D. Matthews, Marwa Helal, Nandi Comer, Gabriel Ramirez, El Williams III, DeAndre Montgomery, Shiyah Troutman, Tyriek White, John Farmer, Luther Hughes, and Raphael Jenkins. To my former loves who served as muses for some of the poems in this collection, thank you for loving me, challenging me, and leaving me to look for another pure love in my life, to quote Stevie Wonder. To the musicians who inspired me through lyric, thank you for laying so many foundations and I hope to keep carrying on the tradition of Black art: The Montclairs featuring Phil Perry, Juicy, Chaka Khan, Tower of Power, Soul II Soul, and D'Angelo. To Black radio stations (especially 92.7 WDZZ) and the DJs who keep me company at night, thank you for keeping Black music moving.

Thank you to my agent, Julia Eagleton, and my editor, Todd Portnowitz, for ushering in another contribution to the field and the culture wars. To Deb Harrison, thank you for your advice; I'll never forget that conversation. Thank you to Harvard's Woodberry Poetry Room for selecting this book for the Creative Fellowship.

Thank you to everyone at Knopf / Penguin Random House for your work on this book.

To the readers, teachers, students, and editors, I hope you all enjoy!

All Gratitude.

1 Love,

J

A NOTE ABOUT THE AUTHOR

Jonah Mixon-Webster is a poet and conceptual/sound artist from Flint, Michigan. His debut collection, *Stereo(TYPE),* won the Sawtooth Poetry Prize and the PEN/Joyce Osterweil Award for Poetry and was a finalist for the Lambda Literary Award for Gay Poetry. He graduated from Eastern Michigan University and received a PhD in creative writing from Illinois State University. He is the recipient of the Windham Campbell Prize for Poetry and fellowships from the Vermont Studio Center, the Center for African American Poetry and Poetics, the Conversation Literary Festival, and the PEN Writing for Justice Program.

A NOTE ABOUT THE TYPE

This book was set in Arno, a typeface designed by Adobe principal designer Robert Slimbach in 2007. Its namesake is the Arno River, which flows through Florence, the city at the heart of the Italian Renaissance. Inspired by the humanist letterforms of the fifteenth and sixteenth centuries, Slimbach designed Arno with the vitality and readability of Venetian and Aldine book typefaces in mind.

Composed by North Market Street Graphics,
Lancaster, Pennsylvania

Designed by Marisa Nakasone